Coming Out
Scene 1

(Megan and Carl are present.)
Carl: Hey Megan, do you want to go hiking this weekend? Since we are both done our first year of university, we might as well spend time together.
Megan: Sorry, I have already started my spring class a week ago. Actually, I'm taking two of them. So I have to study.
Carl: Oh, that's too bad. Maybe in the summer when you are done spring class.
Megan: Sure, but I have to work full time during the summer. I have to work to save up for my tuition for next year.
Carl: Oh, it sounds like you are busy. That's too bad.
        Megan: what program are you in Carl?
Carl: I'm in the bachelor of commerce. I want to be an economist.
Megan: I'm in the bachelor of sciences.
Carl: What do you want to do?
Megan: I want to go to med school to become a doctor.
Carl: Oh, good luck. I better get going. Maybe, we can FaceTime each other once a week to catch up.
Megan: Okay, that sounds good.
Carl: Well, I'm going to go back to my dorm now.
Megan: Okay.

Scene 2

(Carl is at a dorm room with his room mate, Rod.)

Rod: Hi Carl, are you planning to take any spring classes?
Carl: I was going to take the four months off.
Rod: Why don't you take one spring course just to get it out of the way, so that you don't have to take that course in the next school year. I'm taking calculus this spring. I am also doing physics.
Carl: Oh, that sound's heavy. I hate calculus and physics. What level are your courses?
Rod: I am taking both 200levels. That way, I only have to do four per term next year. Actually, I think that I should do three per term instead. I have to work a lot next year.
Carl: I think that I will take a macro economics course. I only took micro economics last term.
Rod: Oh, so are you an economics major?
Carl: Yes, I have already declared my major for my second year. I'm going to minor in marketing.
Rod: Good luck. It's been a pleasure having you as my roommate. You're fun to hang out with and you really take school seriously. I had roommates that just wanted to party. I hate going to bars and clubs. They're so crowded and there are people that just want to drink until they're drunk.
Carl: thank you Rod. I hate doing that to. I find that a lot of people our age are so immature. They act like they're in high school. So Rod, are you going to be staying in the dorms next year?
Rod: No, I'm going to be living an apartment. The rent is cheaper than living in the dorms.
Carl: Oh, congratulations Rod.
Rod: Thanks carl. Hey, let's get in touch by exchanging our phone numbers.
Carl: Okay, that sounds great.

Rod: I guess this is our last day living together. Good luck with Economics.

Carl: Good luck with calculus. I found that class to be difficult. All those derivatives make me mad.

Rod: I scored an A in calculus and physics, but I only scored a C in both my English classes and a B in biology.

Carl: how many classes did you take?

Rod: I took four per semester. I took two classes in the spring before starting my first year.

Carl: How is that possible?

Rod, well, I took a year off to save up for school after I finished high school. I worked three jobs for a year. I applied to start in the spring. This is because I don't want to do five courses per semester in my first year.

Carl: Why did you take a year off?

Rod: It's because I wanted to make sure I had enough money saved up for university. I don't want to have to take out a student loan.

Carl: How many classes are you taking next year?

Rod: Three classes a term. This is because I have to work to pay rent. I don't have time for four or five classes per term. I could not work during my first year. My mom offered to pay my rent for a year. It's really nice of her, but I have to start paying my own rent when I get an apartment. I feel bad when she pays for me. I always worked in high school, but I never put money toward university back then. In Grade twelve, I wanted to go after high school, but I didn't have the money to. So I took a year off.

Carl: Wow, your parents must have taught you money management skills.

Rod: Yes they did. Ever since I was a child, my parents always taught me that I should work for my own money. They also told me not to buy things that I couldn't afford. When I wanted something, I had to save for it.

Carl: Wow, you sure are more mature than me. How old are you?

Rod: I am twenty years old.

Carl: You don't seem twenty years old. I seriously thought that you were twenty-five or twenty-six. You act mature for your age. I want to learn to be like you Rod. I am terrible with money management. I have to take out a student loan because I can't afford it. My parents feel like since it is my education, I have to pay for it. University is so expensive.

Rod: Oh, that's too bad.

Carl: Rod, can you please teach me how to manage my money properly?

Rod: I'll be glad to give you tips on it. After all, my parents raised me to manage my money.

Carl: I'll miss you Rod. (Rod and Carl exchange contact information.)

Scene 3

(Carl and his mom, Juliet are having coffee at a Tim Horton's.)

Carl: Hi mom, how are things going?

Juliet: Things are going fine. How was your first year of university?

Carl: For the most part, it was a good experience. However, the thing I hate is studying for midterms and finals. My professors expect a lot. It's different from high school.

Juliet: Well, I know what that's like. When I went to university to become a high school teacher, I had to do that to. It just takes a while to adjust to university life. It's going to be difficult at times, but I know you can do it son.

Carl: Think you for being so encouraging mom. I really appreciate it.

Juliet: You're welcome son. How are your professors?

Carl: They're okay. They just like to throw information at us.

Juliet: That's what a lot of professors do son. You have to learn a lot on your own.

Carl: I learned that the hard way through my first year of university.

Juliet: So, are you doing anything this spring and summer?

Carl: I'm going to be taking a spring class. I'm also going to work more hours at my job when my spring class is over.

Juliet: I'm very proud of you son.

Carl: I want to be like my roommate, "Rod", who works to save money for school. Right now, I just work on weekends.

Juliet: Just let me know if you need help paying some of your tuition. I'm very proud of you for getting good grades and having a GPA of 3.0.

Carl: Thank you. So mom, do you want anything to drink? I'll buy it.

Juliet: Thank you, that's very generous of you. I would like a medium ice cap. What did you get?

Carl: I got a medium Double Double.

Juliet: I'm so proud of you wanting to save up for school, you are a young man.

Carl: Thank you. I find it a little difficult to manage money in university. There are things to pay for such as my tuition, fees, and textbooks. University is so expensive.

Juliet: Since your GPA is high, why don't you start applying for scholarships? They may help you to pay for some of the costs. It is better than taking out a student loan because you don't have to pay back scholarships.

Carl: That's what I am going to do. Thank you for the suggestion. So Mom, do you want to go shopping after our coffee?

Juliet: Yes, I would love to. some nice clothes would be nice. Good luck in your spring class son.

Carl: Thank you. (Carl exits. Then, he comes back with an ice cap..) Here mom. (He hands it over to her.)

Juliet: Thank you.

Carl: I added a shot of vanilla because I know you like it. Well mom, let's go shopping after our coffee. (Both mother and son drink their coffee. Then, they exit.)

Scene 4

(Carl is in a university classroom with other students. Professor Andrews has the smart board out. On the smart board is the syllabus.)

Professor Andrews: Hello, welcome to Economics 102. On the smart board is the syllabus. You can find this on our course website called "BlackBoard". My name is Professor Andrews, but you can also call me by my first name. You can call me "Professor Andrews" if you are uncomfortable calling me "Mike". First, we will spend a little bit of time going over the syllabus. Do you have any questions? (Carl raises his hand.) Yes?

Carl: Professor, is the final cumulative?

Professor Andrews: Yes it is. I'll talk about that while we go through the syllabus. First, this course covers sixteen chapters. The textbook for our course is listed below. Please do not get the one with the access code because I will not be using Applia. All the assignments and quizzes will be on BlackBoard. (Another student raises her hand.) Yes Cori?

Cori: Professor, I looked at the syllabus and it doesn't say when we are writing our final. It says "TBA". What does "TBA" mean?

Professor Andrews: It means "to be announced".

Scene 5

(Carl and Megan are at his dorm.)
Megan: Hey Carl, how are your spring classes going?
Carl: It's going well Megan. Things are okay. I just started the first two chapters.
Megan: Oh, that's good.
carl: I had no idea that a course in the spring was going to be intense. I'll have to get used to it. It's going to be heavy.
Megan: You'll get used to it. Wow, do you know what day it is?
Carl: It's June the second.
Megan: Yes, but it's also our first anniversary of the day we started dating.
Carl: Oh, I didn't realized that. How did you remember that?
Megan: Well, I had it marked on my calendar for every year on my IPhone, so that I wouldn't forget.
Carl: That is very nice of you. I really don't think that it's a big deal. It's not like we are married.
Megan: Have you ever thought about us getting married in the future?
Carl: Know, I haven't. I think that it's much too soon for that. I just want to focus on finishing university first.
Megan: Okay, that's understandable. Let's go out for our anniversary. Maybe to a fancy restaurant.
Carl: I was thinking about going out to eat sushi. My mom's friend makes it.
Megan: Okay, I love sushi.
Carl: That's good. I was afraid that you would hate it. Most of my high school friends hate sushi because they hate raw fish.
Megan: Well, not all sushi has raw fish. California rolls and cucumber rolls don't have any raw fish.
Carl: That's my favourite. My second favourite is Sushimy.
Megan: So, shall we go with our plan to eat sushi?
Carl: That sounds great. I just have to study. My midterm is in nine days.
Megan: I have to study for my finals. Man, spring classes are so stressful.
Carl: I know. I feel your pain. That's life of a university student.
Megan: Well, let's get studying together. (They both get ready to study. They start reading their textbooks.)

Scene 6

(Carl is in the classroom with Professor Andrews and other students. Professor Andrews is drawing a graph on the smart board.)
Professor Andrews: The graph that I am drawing is the aggregate supply graph. As you can see, the aggregate demand curve slopes down While the aggregate supply curve slopes up. The money supply curve is vertical.
Carl: Cori, I find these graphs a little harder than Micro Economics..
Cori: I feel confused too.
Professor Andrews: Remember that the money supply does not have an effect during the long run. The horizontal axis is able "quantity" while the vertical axis is labeled "interest rate". (Carl raises his hand.)
Carl: (Raising his hand.) Professor, while is the demand curve sloping down while the supply curve slopes up?
Professor Andrews: This is because the model says that demand decreases while supply goes up. When the supply goes down, demand goes up.

Carl: Thanks Professor, that makes sense.

Scene 7

(Carl and his mom, Juliet, are at their home. They are sitting across from each other on opposite sides of the dining table. They are in the living room.)

Juliet: Hi Carl, how was your date with Megan?

Carl: It was good. We both went to eat at a sushi restaurant.

Juliet: Yum, the sound of food in general makes me hungry.

Carl: After we ate, I took her to a jurally shop to pick out a promise ring for her.

Juliet: Oh, that's very nice of you. Does she like it?

Carl: Yes she does. She says that it's pretty.

Juliet: She must be so lucky to have you.

Carl: Yes she is. Mom, I have something to tell you. I've kept it a secret ever since I was in Junior High.

Juliet: What is it son? I'm here to listen to whatever you have to say. No matter what, I'll support you one hundred percent.

Carl: I am gay. I am attracted to boys. I feel like dating a girl doesn't feel right. I feel like I've been lying to myself into thinking that I wanted a girlfriend.

Juliet: (Surprised.) Oh, I never knew that about you. I thought that you were into girls. Well, if that's who you are attracted to, then that's what it is.

Carl: I'm scared to tell dad. He doesn't like gay people. He's bias towards them.

Juliet: I know. I try to get him to open his mind, but he is just ignorant and stubborn. It was hard after we got divorced two years ago, but that's what we had to do. We began to fight a lot.

Carl: Wow, that must feel rough.

Juliet: He's not the kind of man that I thought he was. He always belittled me after I went against his bias opinions against LGTBQ people. He's very closed minded and conservative. He things, "I'm the king, I rule this house". He wouldn't even let me hang out with my friend, Robyn because she was lesbian.

Carl: That's the reason I am so fucking scared mom. I'm scared as heck.

Juliet: Well, you have to try to take a stand. If he doesn't like it, too bad. I know it's hard, but we just have to have the courage to do it. I'll be at your side as a back up. Remember that I am very supportive of you being gay.

Carl: Thanks mom, you are the best.

Juliet: I learned about LGTBQ people in sociology. I even watched a document about Gay people speaking out against prejudice.

Carl: I thank God and Jesus for giving me a mom like you. What would I do without you?

Juliet: That's very sweet of you to say. Did you tell your friends and your girlfriend about this?

Carl: Well, I only told one friend, Rod. He is cool with it. He also doesn't judge. However, my girlfriend doesn't know yet. So do my other friends.

Juliet: Just tell them whenever you're ready son. However, if I were you, I would tell my girlfriend about this first. If you don't tell her soon, she's going to be really confused if she sees you making out with another guy. If you tell her about it and explain everything, she won't be as confused.

Carl: The problem, however, is I don't know how to tell her. I just don't know what to say.

Juliet: Well, remember to think about what you are going to say to her. Write it down on paper. You're an adult now, so it's really up to you about how you are going to tell her.

Carl: Okay, thanks for the advice. That's what I'll do mom.

Juliet: Not a problem son. Anytime. Remember that if you need to talk, I'm always here to listen. I won't judge you.

Carl: Okay mom. I better get back to my dorm to study. I have a midterm in two days.

Juliet: Okay, I wish you all the best on your midterms.

Scene 8

(Carl and Megan are at his dorm sitting next to each other on the bed.)

Carl: Megan, I have something to tell you. I've been keeping it a secret since I was thirteen.

Megan: What is it Carl.

Carl: I am … (He hesitates for a few seconds.) I am gay.

Megan: (Shocked and confused.) What? I'm confused. I don't know what else to say.

Carl: Look, I was scared to confess because I was afraid that other people would hate me for being gay. So I dated girls because I felt like I needed to be attracted to girls. My dad hates gay people. This is why I'm scared to tell him.

Megan: Why didn't you tell me before? I would have been okay with us just being friends. It's not healthy to hide everything. Also, it doesn't do anything to lie to yourself.

Carl: We'll just have to break up. I feel attracted to men. I don't have any sexual attraction towards women. That's just not who I am.

Megan: Break up? I don't want us to break up. We've been going out for a year. I was planning to marry you in a few years and start a family together. This is going to be hard to imagine you dating another guy. I thought the entire time that you were sexually attracted to women.

Carl: Yes, we have to break up. This just doesn't feel right for me. I'm finding a guy to date.

Megan: Well, if that's what makes you happy, I have to respect your wishes. This is going to be very emotional for me. I'm going to miss you.

Carl: We can still be friends Megan.

Megan: We can't just be friends. I still want to be your girlfriend. Someday, I want to be your wife. You're the most mature guy I've ever dated. You taught me quite a lot, such as overcoming test anxiety. Most guys I have dated over the past were wusses. They're like little boys trapped in a body of a twenty-two year old. On the other hand, you are very mature for a nineteen year old in general. My parents would be so impressed if I was dating a guy like you. You are the top one percent of guys I will date. I have rejected at least ninety-nine percent of guys that asked me out because most of them would try too hard to impress me and act like Prince Charming.

Carl: I appreciate your compliment, but it's time for us to say goodbye and move on. We can still talk to each other. The truth is I just want to find a man to date.

Megan: Who did you tell besides me?

Carl: I told my parents and my old roommate, Rod. My mom and Rod are very supportive, but my dad isn't. He says that gay sons are not allowed in his castle. He also said that I am supposed to like girls and not guys because I am a guy. He called me names like faggot, sissy, effeminate, and wuss. He had being berating me on the phone and text messages everyday. He has left very hurtful voice mails on my answering machine, such as the one where he said that he was going to kill me if his son turned out gay.

Megan: Oh my goodness, I feel so bad for you. It sounds like to me that your dad is very berating and degrading.

Carl: My dad also belittles me. He says that I'm acting like a baby and that I'm big now. I want to move out because I don't want to deal with this. I'm also planning to change my cell phone number. I'm going to get a new phone on a new contract. I'm only going to tell my mom about this. I want her to keep it a secret.

Megan: You can block him from calling you. You don't have to change numbers. Just find your dad's contact and tap "block this caller".
Carl: Thanks Megan. I didn't know that you can do that. Well, I guess is time for our goodbye. (Megan starts to sob. She is very emotional.)
Megan: (Sobbing.) I'll miss you! I just feel heartbroken about us breaking up!
Carl: Try not to cry. This is just something we have to face in life. We must go our separate ways so we can grow as persons.
Megan: (Still sobbing.) You're right, but I feel like this happened too fast! (She exits sobbing continuously.)

Scene 9

(Carl in in the living room with his mom, Juliet, and his dad, Garry.)
Carl: (To Garry.) Dad, I don't understand why you are berating me and calling me names? Why can't you accept your own son for being gay?
Garry: (Angry and yelling.) Look, you are not allowed to be gay! I raised you to be a man and men are attracted to women! You are acting like a sissy! Man up! You can't be a sissy boy anymore!
Carl: (Angry.) Look dad, I don't know what your problem is! I don't like your attitude towards gay people! It is degrading and insulting to me!
Garry: Look, you need to grow out of this! You're not a kid! You're an adult already!
Juliet: (Firm, but still calm.) Garry, this is no way to treat our son. I'm not going to allow you to talk to him like this. This is who he is.
Garry: Shut the fuck up Juliet! Our son needs to learn his lesson! He has no manhood because he is a faggot! He's a loser and he deserves to be dead! He's not a "man", he's an "it"!
Carl: I heard that! I'm not deaf!
Juliet: (Angry.) Garry, that is enough! This talk about our son is unacceptable! What kind of a father are you? What kind of a husband are you? You better apologize to Carl now! It hurts his feelings when you say that in front of him! You know what, get out of here now!
Garry: No, this is my house and I make the rules!
Juliet: No, Carl and I moved out before we divorced! I bought my own house and I pay the mortgage! It's not even under your name! Get out of here! I don't every want to see you again! I am going to report your abusive and degrading text messages to the authorities! How dare you have the obdassity to treat our son that way! You're not the king of this house! Since I bought the house with my mortgage and I pay it off, I'm the queen! (Garry exits. Carl becomes upset.)
Carl: I hate dad! I want to tell him "casse toi"! He is a "filse de pute"! I wish that he did not even exist!
Juliet: Look, I hope that you don't call a French person that. If you're taking French, don't say that in front of your French Professor.
Carl: You no French?
Juliet: Well, I know some. I took French from Junior High through High School. Wen I went to Quebec, I would hear people say it. I brought my French speaking friend, Francois, with me. I asked him what the words meant. He told me that they were swear words. He was pretty much my translator. I wish I could speak French fluently like him. Just do not say it in front of Francois. He hates hearing people swear in French. He doesn't do it because he feels that it's bad.
Carl: I never met him. I promise that I won't do it in front of Francois.
Juliet: Now, let's get back on topic. I know your dad is not a nice person. You don't have to see him anymore because I'm going to make sure that he never comes here again. I'm going to sell

this house and move to a condo. It would be cheaper and I just can't afford to keep this house anymore. Don't worry, I will make sure that he doesn't know about it.

Carl: Okay.

Juliet: The good news is that you get to meet Francois. He lives in the same condo building that we will be staying in.

Carl: (Excited.) Great! he can teach me French! I always wanted to learn French!

Scene 10

(Carl in in a professor's office. Professor Andrews and Carl are sitting on the opposite side of the desk.)

Carl: Professor, I failed the second midterm.

Professor Andrews: No you didn't. you got a sixty-five percent on it. Why are you saying you failed?

Carl: I did not get a seventy-five percent like I did on the first midterm. That's going to ruin my GPA. I'm going to look like a failure.

Professor Andrews: Carl, as a professor, I hate to see students beat themselves up like this. A sixty-five percent is no fail. It's almost a C+.

Carl: I would kill myself after getting a sixty-five percent. I don't deserve to be here. I deserve to die Professor.

Professor Andrews: (Concerned.) It worries me when you say that. I suggest you get counselling. I think you need professional help. (Carl exits the professor's office. Professor Andrews follows him.)

Carl: Professor, why are you following me?

Professor Andrews: I'm really worried about what you just said. I take it really seriously when students say that. I'm going to report this to the Student Life Office.

Carl: But Professor, it would be no use.

Professor Andrews: I rather see you get help than seeing you dead. I'm not leaving until I take you to the Student Life Office. Look, I don't want you to end your life so soon. Didn't you say that you wanted to be an Economist?

Carl: Yes Professor.

Professor Andrews: Look, I want you to continue to live so that you can become what you want to be. you are only nineteen years old. It is much too soon for you to end your life.

Carl: Yes Professor. (Professor Andrews and Carl exit.)

Scene 11

(Carl in in his dorm. he is on FaceTime with Rod.)

Carl: Hi Rod, how are classes?

Rod: They are going well. How was your day?

Carl: It was terrible. I got really depressed because I did not get a B or A on my second midterm. I got a C. I even told the professor that I wanted to die.

Rod: Oh my goodness, that does not sound good.

Carl: My professor would not stop following me. He eventually reported it to the Student Life office. He kept insisting me to go there for help.

Rod: It sounds like this professor cares. You're lucky to have a professor like that. In the future, you will have professors that don't care. They won't even know you. I think that you scared your professor when you said that. That's why he's really concerned for you.

Carl: But what do I do so that I don't scare him?

Rod: Just ry not to say what you said.
Scene 12

(Juliet and Carl are in his dorm.)
Juliet: Carl, why on Earth would you tell your professor that you wanted to die? I think you're crazy!
Carl: I don't deserve to be here. I don't even deserve honours at my university. Thanks to that 65%, my GPA will be ruined.
Juliet: Now, try not to make a big deal about it. A 65% on your midterm will not affect your GPA that much. All that I expect is for you to do the best you can. Don't beat yourself up over a 65%.
Carl: That was what my professor tried to tell me.
Juliet: Well, your professor is right. He really doesn't want to see you upset just because you didn't get a grade that you were satisfied with. Do you understand?
carl: Yes mom.
Juliet: You only have one life and try to enjoy what it has to offer. You're too young to end your life.
Carl: The thing is that I don't want to exist anymore. I'm better off dead.
Juliet: That really concerns me. What I suggest is talking to a councillor at school. It's very important to take care of your mental health. I need you to promise yourself that you will seek professional help.
Carl: Okay mom.
Juliet: (Passing a sticky note to Carl.) Here is a number for the distress line. It's open 24/7.
Carl: But mom, what good will it do to talk to someone on the distress line?
Juliet: It will help with your suicide thoughts and how to develop strategies to overcome them. Personally, when I was a teenager, I learned how to make a plan on preventing suicide. Your grandparents became alcoholics when I was five years old. When I was ten, I had a sister with FASD. I was forced to look after her whenever your grand parents went out.
Carl: Oh, that's hard. When did you leave Grandma and Grandpa?
Juliet: I left when I was sixteen. I wanted a better life and I didn't want to become an alcoholic like my mom and dad.
Carl: That is a difficult situation you went through.
Juliet: Now, I want you to promise me that you will call the distress line. I'm not leaving until you do.
Carl: Okay mom.
Juliet: (Patting Carl on the back.) That's my son. Try to have a better day tomorrow. Okay?
Carl: Okay mom, I'll try. Goodnight mom.
Juliet: Good night. Here's my advice to you. Now that you are living on campus, you must take care of yourself. Please don't try to attempt to kill yourself. I will miss you so much if you did. You know that breaks my heart. Please take your professor's advice too. Stay out of trouble.
(Juliet kisses her son on the cheek. Then, Carl calls the distress line number on his cell. Juliet exits the dorm.)

Scene 13

(The scene is in the office of Professor Andrews. The professor is surrounded by ten students.)
Cori: Professor, we have really bad news to tell you. It's unfortunately really depressing.
Professor Andrews: What's the news?
Francis: Professor, I found Carl hung to the ceiling of the Chemistry lab. So, I called 911. Cori was there too. (The professor starts to become emotional. He remains emotional throughout the

scene.) I asked her to check if he was breathing. I told her to do CPR until the ambulance got here.

Cori: I found a piece of paper in his pocket. It was a suicide note (Cori shows the professor the paper.) That was when I knew that he attempted suicide. When I checked up on him, he appeared to not be breathing. Another young man came in and volunteered to wait for the ambulance. (She points to Zack.)

Zack: That is correct Cori. I was just getting ready to do my Chemistry lab. As I entered, I saw a young man, who appeared to be unconscious. (The professor takes a bundle of tissues and blows his nose. He starts to wipe his tears.) I saw Cori doing CPR and Francis calling the ambulance. The rest of us are my classmates from Chemistry 101. My name is Zack and I just met Francis and Cori in the lab this morning. I had to tell my Chemistry professor what was going on. The look on his face was shock and fear. He had to cancel the lab experiment. We all had to guide the ambulance to the lab.

Cori: about a few hours later, I got a call from Juliet that Carl could not be saved. I'm sorry professor, Carl is dead. You did the best you could to help him professor. Juliet is sad too. I know that this is really hard. (Cori tries to comfort the professor.)

Francis: We did our best to help him by trying to revive him and getting an ambulance to the hospital, but it was too late. I'm very sorry too professor. We're all sorry that there was nothing else we could do. (The professor continues to cry. Two more professors come in. One is a tall woman and another is a tall man. The man is Professor Richardson and the woman is Professor Ivy.)

Professor Ivy: Professor Andrews, why are you so upset? (Professor Andrews is unable to contain his composure in order to reply to Professor Ivy.)

Professor Richardson: Now now, it's very unprofessional to be emotional in front of your students.

Cori: : Oh, who are you guys. (She faces the two other professors.)

Professor Ivy: I'm Professor Ivy.

Professor Richardson: And I am Professor Richardson. I was the chemistry professor that had to cancel the lab. I saw what happened too.

Zack: (Facing Professor Richardson.) Professor? What are you doing here?

Professor Richardson: Well, Professor Ivy and I came to see if everything was okay. But when we came in, we did not expect Professor Andrews to be this upset.

Professor Ivy: I'm also a chemistry professor. When I came in the chemistry lab, there was blood on the floor. Also, there was an open bottle of hydrochloric acid and a syringe filled with morphine. I just saw Carl when he was still alive. That was before Professor Richardson had his Chemistry class. What I did was see Carl about to drink hydrochloric acid. I told him not to do it. I took it away from him before he could do it. Then, he walked out of the lab. That was the last time I saw him.

Professor Richardson: (Handing a syringe to Professor Ivy.) Look, I found this in Carl's pocket. It was in the same pocket as the suicidal note. Is this the syringe that you saw?

Professor Ivy: Yes.

Professor Richardson: Did you see him take the syringe with him?

Professor Ivy: No, I didn't notice him doing that.

Professor Richardson: I'm suspecting that he could have hung himself before killing himself with morphine. I found him unconscious already when I entered the lab. I was shocked and scared. When Zack and I found the syringe, it was already empty. The plunger was completely pushed in. However, the needle was still attached.

Zack: (Facing Professor Richardson.) Do you think that he would have done that Professor?

Professor Richardson: I'm afraid so Zack. I'm going to get some doctors to dissect his body to see if there were traces of morphine.

Professor Ivy: When did you find out that Carl was dead?

Professor Richardson: One of the students told me in an email.

Professor Ivy: How did you first react when you saw the syringe?

Professor Richardson: Well, I was scared, especially after I saw the needle that was attached to it. At first, I did not know why he had it. Now that you told me that it had morphine in it, it makes sense that he could have used the syringe to kill himself. He must have filled it with morphine. Then, he could have injected it into himself so that he wouldn't feel any pain.

Cori: That makes sense Professor.

Professor Richardson: (Facing Professor Ivy.) If there was blood on the floor in the chemistry lab, could have this been Carl's blood?

Professor Ivy: I'm not one hundred percent sure. (Professor Andrews blows his nose while continuing to cry. Professor Ivy's expression becomes sympathetic.) Oh, poor Professor Andrews. You must have did your best. (She hugs Professor Andrews while Professor Richardson hands him more tissues. Professor Andrews starts to sob..)

Professor Andrews: (Sobbing.) My best was not good enough! He past away too soon! I didn't know what else to do!

Professor Ivy: (Comforting Professor Andrews.) I understand how you feel. You did the best you could Professor Andrews. He's in Heaven with God now.

Professor Andrews: (Sobbing.) He was too young Professor Ivy! I can't believe he ended his life so soon! He wanted to be an economist! I felt like I could have done more to stop him from killing himself!

Professor Ivy: You did the best you could. Try not to be hard on yourself.

Professor Richardson: (To Professor Ivy.) Professor Ivy, I sure feel bad for Professor Andrews and the other students that knew this young man. It's such a shame.

Professor Ivy: Yes it is. (Professor Andrews blows his nose again.) I can tell that this is very hard on Professor Andrews. He seems to be sobbing uncontrollably.

Professor Richardson: He seems very emotional. That is totally understandable. No student would want to see their professor cry. (All the students start to cry along with Professor Andrews.) I sure can't stand this. This is just too sad.

Scene 14

(Juliet and Francois are sitting with each other on the couch. Juliet looks sad. Francois is concerned. He speaks in a French accent.)

Francois: Bonjour Juliet, what's the matter?

Juliet: I've lost my son Francois. He's gone for good. He died much too young.

Francois: I'm sorry to hear that. I do have to agree that his life was too short.

Juliet: (Crying.) What am I supposed to do now? It doesn't feel the same without him. (Juliet continues to cry. Francois tries to comfort her.)

Francois: That's very unfortunate. Apparently, we can't go back and time and change the past. All that we can do is change the present and future. It's going to be very hard to get over this. I know how it feels because a family member of mine had died too. Now, she's in heaven. So is your son. He wants to see you one day when you go to Heaven. Remember that God and Jesus has him now. He will rest in peace forever.

Pampered
by Thomas Nguyen

Scene 1

Mom: (On the phone.) Hi, Daisy could not make it to school today because she was out partying last night.

Stephanie: Mom, what on earth are you doing? you baby Daisy too much! She is not a kid! She's in university! Ramon and I always have to work hard while Daisy does nothing! How could you tell Daisy's professor that she was out partying? That is a stupid excuse! (Mom hangs up.)

Mom: Daisy is a child and she'll always be.

Ramon: She is not! I moved out at sixteen and had to work my butt off! If you pamper Daisy too much, she's not going to be ready to transition into adulthood. When is Daisy ever going to have a job? She's eighteen!

Mom: But she's the baby! She doesn't have to do anything!

Stephanie and Ramon: (Together.) She is not a baby!

Ramon: (Angry.) She is in freaking university! What the heck is the matter with you? You're out of you mind! What is Daisy going to do when she moves out? She's probably going to say, "Mom, Dad, can I have money to pay rent?". Daisy needs a freaking job now! If she can't pay for university, that is her problem. Don't be paying for Daisy's freaking university tuition! Make her pay it herself!

Mom: Ramon, stop telling me what to do! And no professing!

Stephanie: Ramon is right mom!

Mom: Don't you start professing too Stephanie!

Stephanie: I am not professing! Give me the damn phone and I will talk to Daisy's Sociology professor!

Mom: No!

Ramon: Give her the freaking phone!

Mom: (Handing the phone to Stephanie.) Fine! (Stephanie phones.)

Ramon: Anyways mom, you should say to Daisy, "If you run out, I don't care! You are going to wait for your pay cheque."

Stephanie: Good day Professor. Sorry to bother you. Can I talk to you for a second? It's about Daisy. She's so lazy and she doesn't even do her homework. She party's too much. (Pauses.) I don't know why she is lazy. Okay, have a good day. (Stephanie hangs up.)

Mom: What the heck did you tell Daisy's Professor? Are you out of your mind?

Stephanie: No, you are! Daisy is a freaking young adult and she also doesn't have a car or Driver's license. Her professor is going to kick her out of the class and she's not going to be allowed to attend the university. I don't think she deserves to go to university

Mom: (Angry.) You kicked her out of university?

Stephanie: It's not my fault, it's her's! Stop spoiling her! (Daisy enters)

Ramon: Daisy, Annebella Jones, you are in serious trouble! Your professor is not letting you back in his class because you are so lazy! You barely attend class and you don't even do your homework!

Daisy: (Rolling her eyes at Ramon.) Are you my father or something? Who made you boss?

Ramon: Young lady, don't be talking to me like that! I'm going to ground you because you were slacking off in your first year of university! When are you ever going to grow up? You're eighteen years old! You can't be acting like a kid anymore!

Daisy: (Curtly.) I don't care!

Ramon: Look, do not talk to me in that tone! I don't appreciate it! Do you want to go back to university or not?

Daisy: Yah, maybe.

Ramon: Is that your answer? From now on, You are going to get a full-time job, find an apartment and move out! You are going to pay your own bills!

Daisy: I'm and adult! You can't be telling me what to do!

Ramon: You just don't get it! Don't you! Being an adult is about responsibility! It's not about freedom! You want something, you work for it! Mommy and Daddy are not paying you bills and cooking for you! You are also going to do your own laundry, pay your credit card and cell phone bill and rent! You are also going to earn your own money! I don't care if you like it or not! That's adulthood for you! I'm twenty years old and I am more mature than you! Stephanie is twenty-four and she already finished university! You have no life because you are a slacker! If you run out of money, you will wait for your pay cheque. Pay your own damn university tuition! I don't care if you go on student loans or not.

Daisy: Student loans? I don't need student loans, mom will pay for university!

Stephanie: Save up for your freaking university! Cook your own damn food! We're not cooking for you!

Ramon: Are you even listening to me? You are so immature, lazy and careless. Sometimes, I just wish that you would goddamn grow up!

Stephanie: By the way Daisy, it's your fault that your professor kicked you out of his class! Not mine! I explained to him that you are freaking lazy and you are not punctual! It's time you grow up!

DaisY: Mom is going to get me what I want and you're not the boss of me!

Ramon: (Angry.) Shut your pie hole and listen up! Stop acting like a spoiled brat! (Ramon gives Daisy a spank.) I am going to tell Mom to kick you out of the house and live on the streets! Wait until you see! Mom is going to realize that her little princess is a freaking spoiled brat who is selfish, lazy, immature and a procrastinator! (Gives Daisy another spank and Daisy cries.) Shut the F up! (Gives another spank. Daisy cries even louder.) Shut up!!!!

Mom: Ramon, stop spanking Daisy!

Ramon: Mom, she deserves it! can't you really see who your little baby princess is? She is a spoiled brat!

Mom: So, she's the baby!

Stephanie: (To Mom.) That excuse is completely unacceptable! Daisy is not learning anything because you spoil her!

Ramon: Mom, please listen to me and learn to be aware of what Daisy is doing to you! She is a stuck up, selfish and lazy spoiled brat! She always relies on you for money and you always get her what she wants! You've turned her into a spoiled brat that she is now! Whenever she does not get what she wants, she will scream, cry and wine like a child. Daisy's professors think that she is an irresponsible student who cannot learn to take responsibility for her actions! She gets freaking damn zeros for not completing her homework.

Mom: (Finally realizing.) I stand corrected Ramon and Stephanie. I apologize for telling you not to profess. I need to stop spoiling Daisy. I was too focused on trying to give her luxury that I didn't realize that I've turned her into a spoiled brat.

Ramon: Thank you for your understanding mom.

Mom: you're welcome. (She faces Daisy wining. She is firm.) Daisy, stop wining and grow up! I am not going to give anything you want anymore! You are going to get it yourself!

Daisy: (Throwing a tantrum like a toddler.) Mom, it's not fair! You're mean! (Daisy walks away.)

Mom: (Raising her voice.) Come back here young lady, you are not going anywhere! Walking away is rude and I am still talking to you!

Ramon: That's it mom, keep doing it. (Ramon follows Daisy while he raises his voice.) Get back here right now! (Daisy runs back and rolls her eyes at Mom.)

Mom: Daisy, it's rude when you roll your eyes at me! I am trying to tell you that life is not fair! Now learn how to act like a young adult! I am not going to pay your university tuition anymore if you choose to go back! I don't think that you are mature enough to go to university and I am so disappointed that you let your professors down! You need to take responsibility for you actions because no one's going to take responsibility for you!

Daisy: But you always get me what I want! Why aren't you doing that anymore? (She continues to whine.)

Ramon: (Angry.) Enough of your f-ing whining! (Ramon kicks Daisy in the but.) F you! Shut up! (Mom and Daisy leave. Ramon and Stephanie talk face to face while sitting on two chairs across the dining table.)

Stephanie: Your side of the debate worked Ramon! Congratulations bro.

Ramon: Thanks. At least mom finally realizes that Daisy needs to grow up. Hey, I have a plan. Daisy can live in my apartment or yours.

Stephanie: Nah, your apartment is too small. You only have a bachelor suite. Not enough for two at all.

Ramon: But the rent is cheaper.

Stephanie: My apartment is bigger and if Daisy lived at my apartment, she can have her own bedroom. I have two bedrooms, a bathroom and a kitchen. She may be a spoiled brat, but she needs some privacy.

Ramon: What is the point of Daisy living with you?

Stephanie: Well, the plan is to tell Daisy that she is going to move out in one month. She is going to live with me after she learns now to be responsible. When Daisy lives with me, I am going to teach her now to manage money, budget, pay bills and shop for groceries. There will be no babying. I think that Mom should make Daisy bus all the time until she at least get's a license. Let's make her get her learners as soon as possible.

Ramon: Good point. If we make Daisy do things herself. She'll realize that we are just trying to teach her how to be an independent individual. Don't forget, Daisy needs to learn the skills for getting a job before we help her look for one.

Scene 2

(Next Day Daisy, Ramon and Stephanie are in a bedroom.)
Ramon: Daisy, Stephanie and I had a long discussion last night in the living room. We are having you live in Stephanie's apartment in a month.
Daisy: (Shocked.) You mean I'm moving out?
Ramon: (Confessing.) Yes, you are going to move out. You're not going to live with mommy and daddy for long. You're an eighteen-year-old woman and it's time you leave the nest. You are also going to look for a job, learn how to budget and buy things that you need such as groceries, clothes and personal hygiene items.
Daisy: What do you mean by hygiene?
Ramon: Things to keep yourself clean. For example: shapoo and conditioner, face wash, soap, tooth brushes etc.
Daisy: Why are you making me move out?
Ramon: It's because we want to teach you how to live independently and to experience what being an adult is like. Today, I am going to help you look for a job. Stephanie is going to making you do chores around the house and babysit. She is also going to teach you some job skills, so you can keep your job longer. Mom is not going to help you at all and Stephanie and I are going to ensure that she backs off.
Daisy: Okay. I'll try not to act like a spoiled brat and I am sorry. I'll try to act more mature. (One month later.)
Stephanie: So Daisy, You are going to move out tonight into my apartment. How do you feel about that?
Daisy: I don't know. It sounds pretty challenging.

Stephanie: You'll get use to it. You'll love moving out. Trust me.
Daisy: Is there a lot that I need to pack?
Ramon: Are you excited to move out Daisy?
Daisy: I sure am, but at the same time, I am nervous.
Stephanie: Ramon, can we use your truck to carry Daisy's bed?
Ramon: Sure we can. My truck is big enough.
Stephanie: Yes. You start cleaning out your room with all of your things. Ramon and I will disassemble your bed in a second.

Daisy: Sure. (Daisy gets ready to pack while Stephanie and Ramon get to work on disassembling the bed.)
Stephanie: Daisy, Start packing your possessions. (Daisy begins to pack.)

Scene 3

Ramon: We are all done. now, it is time to say goodbye to mom.
Daisy: Okay.
Stephanie: Do you think that you are ready to leave mom's home?
Daisy: I sure am. (Mom is in the living room sobbing.)
Ramon: Hi mom.
Daisy: Hi mom, I am here to say goodbye. I am moving out today. Don't worry, I'll email you everyday to see how I am doing.Stephanie: Daisy is not living in her own apartment yet. She's living with me. There will be absolutely no babying at all. Daisy will learn the skills to be an independent young adult.
Mom: (Crying.) Oh my goodness, this is happening too fast!
Ramon: Don't worry, you'll get used to it. when Stephanie and I moved out? You were really sad. But just in no time, you got use to it. (Mom hugs Daisy.)
Ramon: Come on mom, it's time to let go of your little baby. She is not a baby. (Mom stops hugging Daisy and the three siblings exit.)

Scene 4

(The scene is in Stephanie's apartment. The walls are painted white and there is furniture.)
Daisy: Gosh, what a lovely apartment Steph!
Stephanie: Thank you. I've never seen you appreciate me before. You were a selfish stuck up person before who only thought about herself.
Daisy: I know and I am sorry. I shouldn't have acted so spoiled and learn that I can't always get what I want. I need to realize that I need to be responsible for myself.
Ramon: (Putting his hand out for a high-five.) Daisy, that was a mature thing you have said. (Gives Daisy a high-five.)

Scene 5

(Two month's later.)
Daisy: Steph, I've got my first pay cheque!
Stephanie: Congratulations. I'm very proud of you.
Daisy: Thank you.
Stephanie: You're welcome. How much did you make?
Daisy: fifteen hundred. I have enough money to help pay rent, buy groceries and pay for my learners!
Stephanie: Don't you see how good it is to work for your money?
Daisy: Yes, I feel independent.

Little Professor

Hello, my name is James and I am in Grade 8. My favourite subjects are math and science. My favourite sciences are chemistry and physics. I can do math up to Grade 10 and my math teacher, Mr. Barns is impressed. However, My Language Arts teacher, Mrs. Klein, does not like math. I'm not even allowed to do math in her class and that is sad.

I have three other friends, John, Liz, and Allen, who also are math geeks. They also like physics, just like I do. All the other kids call us "little professors". We've been called "nerds" in Grade 7.

Today, I'm going to tell you the time we got our math and physics books taken away. It was October of our Grade 8 year. Everyone else was silently reading while my three friends and I sat at the back of Mrs. Klein's class doing trig. All the other kids looked at us with weird looks.

"What is this?" a boy with a hockey shirt asked, pointing to me.

"Trig," I said.

I tried to explain what trig was, but he didn't get it. All of a sudden, Mrs. Klein caught John, Liz, and Allen doing math.

"Guys, you're supposed to be reading, not doing math," she said.

"We are reading, technically. We are problem solving at the same time," John said trying to sound smart.

"There is no math allowed in my class. This is Language Arts, not math class."

After Mrs. Klein walked away from us, we went back to doing trig again. Ten minutes later, she took our math books away and gave us a novel to read instead. After Language Arts was over, we told the math teacher what happened. He felt sorry for us. But at the same time, he told us, "When you want to do math, wait until it's math class."

Our math teacher let's us do trig in his class. He was really impressed that we could do high school math. He even recommended us to join math competitions and start a math club at school.

My friends and I get a 95% average in Mr. Barn's class. We do not like it when we score an 89% or less on tests. Whenever that happens, we beg Mr. Barns for a rewrite. Best of all, he lets us do that.

When other kids struggle in certain questions, such as fractions, geometry, and algebra, they come to me and my friends for help during class and after school. After we started helping them, their grades went from 60's to 80's.

Mr. Barns lets me and my other math friends do difficult math because we find Grade 8 math too easy. After we worked on trig, we started working on graphing linear equations. We know that the general equation of a linear equation is $y = mx+b$. M is the slope and B is the Y intercept. All the other kids get confused when they see this equation. When we showed Mr. Barns what we knew, he praised us.

"Wow, that's pretty high level math for an eighth grader. I'm very proud of my little math children,? he praised.

He watch us graph equations like $y = 3x+2$, $y = -2x+1$, and so on. Other kids looked at us confused.

In November, Mrs. Klein would always tell me and my math friends to give our math books to her. We had no choice but to. During the middle of silent reading, John and I went to Mr. Barns's classroom and told him what happened again. We begged him to give us some back up math work sheets. He kindly gave us an old high school math book that was published in the year 2000. It was still in good condition. We thanked Mr. Barns and went back to Language Arts class. John and I hid the math book in my back pack before entering Mrs. Klein's class. When we entered, she questioned us where we went. We lied to her about Mr. Barns needing to see us about our grades. We didn't want her to know what really happened because we didn't want her taking away the math book that he gave us.

Worse of all, Mrs. Klein gave my friends and I a half hour detention just for doing math in her class. That was not fair. After the detention was over, we went to Mr. Barns and sobbed. He tried to comfort us and offered to stick up for us whenever Mrs. Klein tried to take away our math books again. Finally, he managed to go with us to talk to Mrs. Klein. He told her not to ever take away our math books and let us have them. He also told her to let us do math whenever we are not in Language art's class or if we are done our language arts homework. Surprisingly, Mrs. Klein agreed. So, from now on, we never had to have our math books taken away again.

Next year, my friends and I are transferring to pre-AP. I can not wait because we find the regular curriculum too easy and we need to be challenged. I sure can't wait to take AP when I go to high school because I can earn university credits while in high school.

From Female to Male
by Thomas Nguyen

I'm Thomas
And I was assigned female at birth.
I was confused with my gender identity as a child.
I did not know the difference between a boy and girl.
I remember my mom putting me in a dress as a young child.
I didn't understand why.
While the boys were told to say the months of the year by my Grade One teacher,
I would say it with them.
"You're not a boy, you're a girl," my EA would say.

At nine years of age, I noticed I was growing buds.
I did not know what was going on.
Getting my period at twelve was a disaster.
In the summer of 2005, I knew I wanted to be a boy.
I cut my hair short at fourteen,
But was forced to grow it long.
I was not happy living as a girl.

At age nineteen, I did some research about people like myself.
I realized I was transgender.
I did not have the courage to come out
Until I was twenty-three.
My family and friends were accepting,
But my dad wasn't.
It took him a while to accept that I was transgender.
I changed my name and started wearing boy clothes.
I didn't want my girl clothes anymore.

Now, I get to live as my authentic self, as Thomas.
I am happy that I have support.
Without that, I wouldn't be wear I am now.

Crush

Scene 1

Lina: Hey liz, I just met the cutest guy in school. He's so hot. His eyes are so attractive and he has a handsome smile.
Liz: (Excited.) OMG! Really?
Lina: Yes!
Liz: I think you have a crush on him. Why don't you ask him out?
Lina: I'm too nervous! I don't know if I can do it!
Liz: Ask him out at lunch tomorrow. (Next day.)
Lina: (looking at a guy sitting across from her.)
Liz: Oh my god, this is the guy I've been telling you about. (She points at him.)
Liz: He is good looking. Ask him out now.
Lina: What do I do? This is my first crush!
Liz: Look at him and talk to him. Get to know him a little first.
Lina: (Looking at the guy.) Hi, what's up?

Mike: Not much, just chilling.
Lina: You're hot.
Mike: Thanks.
Lina: Do you have any plans after school?
Mike: Yes, I'm very busy. I have to babysit my brothers and sisters and go to soccer practice.
Lina: What's your name?
Mike: I'm Mike. What is your's?
Lina: I'm Lina. Would you like to go out with me?
Mike: Sure, give me some time to think about it.
Lina: (Excited as she faces Liz.) Did you hear what Mike said?
Liz: Yes I did. He seems like a nice guy.

Scene 2

Lina: Mom, dad, I asked a boy out!
Mom: Good for you Lina! Is he cute?
Lina: Yes he is. His name is Mike. I just asked him out today at lunch.
Dad: Lina, you're fourteen. It's too early for you to date now. Wait until you are in college. You'll meet some hot guys there.
Lina: I'm almost fifteen and I am a sophomore in high school. College is quite a while away dad.
Mom: Come on honey, it's normal for teens to have crushes on guys or girls. Our daughter is going through a boy liking stage.
Dad: Fine, I just hope Lina won't sleep with him.
Mom: I hope so too. I don't want our daughter getting pregnant young. But I hope that guy she asked out is nice.

Dad: Me too. If our daughter ever becomes pregnant, she's toast.

Lina: Trust me, I'm not going to have sex.

Dad: I'm just being a father. It is my job to makes sure that you don't get into any trouble like having sex and drinking.

Lina: I promise I won't. If everyone is doing something that I don't think is right, I promise not to get into peer pressure.

Dad: Okay, have fun on your date. And remember, no sleeping with boys.

Lina: I promise.

Scene 3

Lina: Hi Mike, what's up?

Mike: Not much. Are you enjoying our first date?

Lina: I sure am.

Mike: Would you like me to get you anything to eat?

Lina: Sure. I would like a burger from Burger King.

Mike: Sure, no problem.

Lina: Could you also get me a coke? (Mike exits as Lina is texting. He then enters with a burger and coke.) Thanks Mike.

Mike: No problem. Just being a gentleman. What grade are you in?

Lina: I'm in my sophomore year in high school. What grade are you in?

Mike: I am in Grade Twelve. I'm off to college next year.

Lina: What college are you going to?

Mike: I'm going to the University of Washington. I'm planning to study far away from home.

Lina: Why don't you study here in California?

Mike: Because I like to travel and it would be nice to study far from home. I think that you experience some independence while you study far away.

Lina: Okay, good luck getting accepted in to the University of Washington.

Mike: Thank you.

Lina: I have to go home now. I'll talk to you later.

Mike: Bye Lina.

Scene 4

Liz: So how was your date with Mike?

Lina: It was great. Mike seems like a nice guy. He offered to buy me some lunch.

Liz: That was nice of him. Are you guys planning to go on another date?

Lina: I don't know, I'll phone him and ask him.

Liz: You should, he seems like a decent guy.

Lina: On the phone.) Hi Mike, do you want to go on another date? Okay, no problem. (She hangs up.)

Liz: What did he say?

Lina: He says that he is too busy working, however, he says that we can go on a date next Saturday.

Liz: That's great! Good luck.

mike: Hi lina, I just came to say goodbye. I'm leaving for college in three days.
Lina: Already? This is too fast!
Mike: We can still email and chat on the phone. (Mike gives Lina a piece of paper.)
Lina: Thanks Mike, you're the most caring boyfriend I've ever had.
Mike: Look, let's just be friends. I'm not ready for a relationship yet.
Lina: But you're the only guy I like so far.
Mike: Look, you might change your mind and so will I. Not all guys are decent like I am.

Scene 5:

Liz: Lina, Mike's not really going to the University of Washington. All along, he was faking it. He just left you because he had an affair with another girl.
Lina: But he seems like a nice guy. I can't believe that he would do this!
Liz: When I bumped into him, I asked him if he was really studying at the University of Washington. he told me the whole truth. He kept a secret from you just so he would not hurt your feelings.
Lina: (Angry.) I can't believe it! I went out with a guy who appeared to be decent, but was a jerk behind my back! He is the most dishonest guy I've ever met!
Liz: You should break up with him. No guy has the right to take advantage of you. Next time you meet a guy, get to know him first before you date him.
Lina: I'm confused. He was nice on our date.
Liz: well, he's not the guy you think he is. He is dishonest and selfish. You don't deserve a guy who lies behind your back.
Lina: How did you find out?
Liz, well, some of his friends were saying this. Well, they used to be his friends. I met this kid named Sara during lunch time. It just happens that she is Mike's ex-girlfriend. She broke up with him because he cheated on her behind her back.
Lina: (Disgusted.) Are you serious? This is unbelievable!

Numerator and Denominator

By Thomas Nguyen

You are my numerator, and I am your denominator.

I just cannot equal to zero,

Because that will make the fraction undefined.

The fraction is indeterminate when we are both zero.

We must take it to the limit.

Will the limit go to positive or negative infinity?

Will it go to a finite number?

Our puzzle must be solved.

Living as Your True Self
by Thomas Nguyen

You feel like you have to live a lie during your life.
You feel like a boy.
But when you try to tell your parents,
They don't accept it.
You want to cut your hair short and wear boy clothes.
You find dresses a pain to wear.
You don't have teachers who understand you.
They tell you to act more feminine.

In high school, you try to act more girlly.
You try things like wearing perfume and using purses.
You feel like committing suicide
Because you have no one that understands you.

In University, you have the courage to come out.
You realize that you are transgender.
With support, you decide to transition.
It is not easy.
Changing your name and gender
On your legal documents.
Also, waiting to start on hormones.

You finally have the courage to give away your girl clothes
And start dressing more like a boy.
You have the courage to cut your hair really short.
You finally can live as your true self.

My Friend Brady
by Thomas Nguyen

I have a friend named Brady.
He was a cool person to hang out with.
I met him in high school
When I was in Grade 10.
He reminded me of Terry Fox
Because like him, he struggled with cancer.
I often hung out with him during lunch time.
When I was in Grade 12,
I found out he had died.
I kept my feelings about what had happened to him.
Never had I talked to a lot of people about it.
Well, at least Jesus has him now.

Crush on a Professor
by Thomas Nguyen

Before I started my first year of university, I was intimidated because the course load was going to be heavier than it would be in high school. I was not looking forward to having to pay for my tuition and books. Worse of all, boring professors that would just lecture non-stop. I got a few scholarships, but they only helped pay for three classes. I had to rely on student loans to pay for the rest of the year.

During the summer, I worked to try to earn money for university. However, it was also not enough. tuition at Kings University was too much. At least $20000 per year.

My first day of university was not as boring as I thought. My philosophy professor was interesting. He had a good sense of humour and liked to joke and tease. His name was Henry Davis. What was strange was that he wanted to be called by his first name. In high school, we have to address teachers as Mr. and Mrs. and not their first name.

During the third month of my first year, I started to have a crush on Henry. He seemed very smart and commanding as he lectured. I did not expect that he would be able to tell if I did have a crush on me. One time, he asked me to go to his office to discuss my grade on my midterm. After I followed him to his office, I sat at his table across from him.

"So Professor, can I see my midterm?" I asked.

He quietly passed my midterm back to me. Surprisingly, I got an 80% on it. I was not expecting a mark that high before. Normally, I would get low 70's in Philosophy. I thanked Henry and got ready to go to my chemistry class. As i was leaving, Henry followed me and asked if I could stay a little longer.

"I'm sorry Professor," I said. "I don't want to be late for my chemistry class."

Next, Henry took out a piece of paper and wrote his phone number on it. Then, he passed it to me. I continued to walk to my next class feeling awkward.

During the second semester, Henry asked me to go for coffee with him. I politely accepted his offer and we had coffee in the school cafeteria. When I got ready to go to my dorm during night time, Henry started to become a little overprotective. He offered to walk me home.

"No thinks professor," I politely said. "I can walk home by myself."

"Okay, but please text or call me when you get to your dorm."

I started running to my dorm before the professor could follow me. I found it weird when a professor is overprotective. He was not my father and I didn't understand why he had to hover over me. When I got home, I got right to studying my chemistry notes because I had a midterm on it the next day. Then, I started working on my calculus and physics homework. By midnight, I got a text from Henry and it read: "Bella, did you get home safe?" I replied to the professor's texts and told him that I had to go back to studying.

However, things got worse when Henry forced me to sleep at a hotel with him. I was not comfortable with it at all. However, I felt like since he was my professor, he had power over me. In the hotel room, he touched me inappropriately and I was not okay with it. I wondered to myself, "What should I do?" Whenever I tried to resist, he would not let me go anywhere.

A few months after the incident, I began to notice my belly getting bigger. After I did a pregnancy test, I discovered that I was pregnant. Next, I told Henry about it. However, he denied that he was the father and accused me of sleeping with other men. After I hung up the phone, I began to become emotional because I could not believe that he was a pervert in disguise. After I told a councillor at my university during the first semester of my second year, she suggested that I report it to the Dean.

It took me a lot of courage to tell the dean what was going on. The dean was Dean Henderson. He was tall and wore a suit. When I came into his office, he asked, "How can I help you?"

I began to tell him about the incident with my philosophy professor and the time I was forced to sleep with him at the hotel. The dean was taking notes as I was speaking and took everything I said seriously. He also looked at me with concern.

"How will you be able to finish school after you have the baby?" the dean asked. "You're only eighteen years old. It's too soon for you to have a child."

"I don't think so Dean Henderson," I answered.

Two weeks after I told the dean, I got news from the university that Henry was fired from his job for conducting an inappropriate professor and student relationship with me and five other female students. I was glad that he was fired. What a creep he was! During December of my second year of university, I went into labour and had the baby. It was a boy and he weighed six pounds and five ounces. He looked a lot like Henry. I decided to name my baby Timothy.

I had to drop out of my second semester because I had to take care of Timothy. It was a lot of work and it was not easy being a mother at eighteen. Luckily, my parents supported me and helped me out as much as they could. When I told my friend, Sam about my pregnancy, he offered to get a job to support the baby. A few months after Sam got his own condo, I moved in with him.

Living with Sam was great because he was a very supporting and understanding person. He wanted to do what was best for me and Timothy. I want to go back to school, but it's not possible right now. My baby needs me and I don't want to put him in a daycare yet.

The challenges of being a young mom is taking care of my son and sometimes, it can be hard to put him to sleep. At times, I have to stay up with him and feed him. When I'm tired, Sam helps out with the baby. I breast feed Timothy because I heard that it was the best for the baby. The nurses at Royal Alex hospital encouraged me to do it because babies who are breast fed are less likely to get sick. Timothy is now seven months old and he has put on a lot of weight. He ways fifteen pounds now and he is healthy. I'll wait until my son is two years old before I go back to school because right now, I need to take care of him.

Obsession with Math
by Thomas Nguyen

I love math
And I don't know where my life would be without it.
Math has been my favourite subject
And it will always be.
With my math studies,
I want to get a PhD
And become a math professor.
I used to stay up late doing math.
My math teachers would tell me to get proper rest.
I am so obsessed with math.
I even have π buttons and a π mug.

Overprotective Sociology Professor
by Thomas Nguyen

(The setting is in the classroom with about forty students. The clock reads 9:00.)

Professor Johnson: I hope that you guys have a good night. We are going to talk about social inequality next Wednesday.

Wendy: So David, let's bus home to our apartments.

David: But I hate bussing home, especially by myself. Too bad I have to because I have no ride.

(All the students get ready to leave. Professor Johnson looks at David and Wendy with concern.)

Professor Johnson: So David and Wendy, do you guys have a ride?

David: No, we're busing home by ourselves.

Professor Johnson: Please don't bus home at night. I really recommend that you have a ride.

Wendy: But I live by myself and I am too poor to afford a car. That's why I bus.

Professor Johnson: Do you have a room mate?

Wendy: You're my professor. Why are you asking this? This is weird.

David: Yah Professor Johnson, we need you to please back off! Wendy and I will bus together! Problem solved!

Professor Johnson: i'll drive you guys home.

Wendy: No thanks Professor, we're fine.

David: By the way, I live by myself too!

Wendy: Come on David, lets go. (David and Wendy leave with the other students.

David: Man, our sociology professor is so overprotective! I wish that he would back off. (David and Wendy leave the university to catch their bus.)

Wendy: Our bus should be here soon. I just home that our professor won't hover over us. (The bus arrives. David and Wendy get on the bus.)

Wendy: Finally, no more overprotective professor for now! (David's phone rings. David answers it.)

David: Hello, why are you calling me? (David pauses.) Yes, now can you please back off? Goodbye. (David hangs up.)

Wendy: Who was that?

David: It was our professor. Man he is getting on my nerves!

Wendy: Man, that was just weird. I don't think that it's any of his business to try to get into our personal lives. He's not our father; he's our professor.

David: I know. What is he going to do than? Watch us get on the bus after we walk to the bus stop? This is freaking me out! (David's phone rings again. David answers.) Hello Professor Johnson. (He pauses.) Why do I need to call you when we get home? (He pauses again. This time, he is frustrated.) Seriously? Back off Professor Johnson! You're so overprotective! (David hangs up)

Wendy: Man, I hate this professor! He's going too far!

David: I'm going to tell the dean if he keeps doing it. I'm going to switch to another sociology class.

Wendy: Let's get off at my place. It's closer.

David: Okay. (David's phone makes a tri tone sound. He gets a text message.)

Wendy: Who is the text from?

David: It's our professor. He just wants to know if we got home yet.Wendy: What am I going to do with him? He's not our parent!

David: I know. (David's phone receives a second text message. David looks at the second message.) Man, not our professor again!

Wendy: What did he say?

David: He says, "Why aren't you replying? I'm getting worried."

Wendy: Man, I hate him!

David: Me too! If I reply, he better back off! (David replies to the professor's text message.)

Wendy: What are you going to tell him?

David: I am going to tell him not to call and text me anymore. I am going to block him so that he can't call me anymore.

Wendy: Isn't that too harsh David?

David: No, he deserves it because he is invading our privacy.

Wendy: Are we going to go with your plan to switch to another sociology class?

David yes. (David and Wendy arrive at Wendy's apartment building. They get off the bus and head to her apartment. On the next day, they are at the university cafeteria.)

Wendy: Hey David, did you manage to switch to another sociology class?

David: Yes I did. Did you?

Wendy: Yes, I did to. I managed to switch to a day time class. I'm not with the overprotective sociology professor anymore.

David: Me too, I am so annoyed and frustrated with him. (Professor Johnson approaches David and Wendy in the cafeteria.)

David: What do you want Professor?

Professor Johnson: I heard you guys say things like how overprotective I am. I may be overprotective, but I'm just looking out for you.

David: Frustrated.) Yah, by calling me and texting me for the first two weeks! You're not my father; you are my professor! We just want you to back off because we need our own space!

Wendy: This is why we switched to another sociology class because we didn't want to deal with you! You are the most overprotective professor that I ever had! What you did was inappropriate! Goodbye Professor! (David and Wendy exit.)

Adult Children
by Thomas Nguyen

When my daughter, Ashley, was twenty years old, I tried to get her to move out because she barely did anything around the house. She often left messes in the kitchen and expected me to clean up after her like she was a kid. It was hard to get her to follow my rules because she often disrespected my house hold. All she did was sleep in and go out. She couldn't even hold a job and was fired after three months.

Ashley often partied and came home drunk. She dated a boyfriend who was much older than her. He was at least forty years old and he sold drugs. One time when I came home, she was not home yet. It was 2:00 A.M and I was worried sick for her. When I called her, she picked up the phone. I asked where she was and I wanted her home immediately.

"You're not the boss of me mom," she screamed. "I can do whatever I want and I don't need a bitch like you to tell me what to do."

"Listen Ashley," I said. "I need you to get your shit together. If you don't, you will mess up yourself in the future. I don't want you to be with your boyfriend anymore because he's too old for you. You're a kid. He's an adult and he doesn't make good choices."

She then began to scream, "I'm not a kid! you can't tell me what to do!" I firmly told her that this was my house and that she was going to follow the rules. I tried punishments such as grounding her and taking her electronics away, but nothing seemed to be working. My husband, Sam and I were so fed up with her and we decided that she should move out.

"You think you're so grown-up now," Sam yelled to Ashley. "Git your butt here and pack your stuff! If you don't follow our rules, you can't stay here!"

After we managed to get our twenty-year-old daughter out of the house, we told her that she was not welcomed back until she learned to respect us and our rules. After she left, we finally had peace and quiet to ourselves. It felt good to get her to leave the house and live somewhere else. My husband and I hoped that she would learn her lesson.

Ashley was not always so disrespectful. From the time she was in elementary and Junior High, she always did her homework and followed the house rules. She sometimes offered to help out with the house chores. She used to babysit her little cousins after school. I do miss the old Ashley and I really want her back.

When she was in High School, she began to hang out with the wrong people and made friends with them. She was pressured by them to take drugs, smoke, and skip classes. I often received calls from her school that said that she was absent and missing classes. I discussed this situation with her frequently, but she didn't seem to care. She was not herself. In Grade 11, she dropped out of school and did drugs. I was so mad at her.

After she moved out, I still worried about her. I've been calling her on the phone multiple times a day and suggested that she should get help with her drug addiction. Many times, she refused to, but I didn't want her to die from doing drugs. It took her months to realize that she needed to quit doing drugs. When I first took her to the rehab centre, she resisted going there. However, I kindly told her, "You need help and I want you to learn how to overcome your addiction because I want you to be healthy. Listen, I love you and I don't want anything to happen to you." I called a rehab centre and I requested to get an addictions counsellor for Ashley. It took her a year to overcome her addiction and she started to learn how to make better decisions. She decided that she wanted to go back and upgrade so that she could get her high school diploma. In months, she was back to her old self. She decided to break up with her boyfriend because after she quit drugs, he began to beat and rape her. He tried to force her to go back and do drugs. About four months after she broke up with him, she discovered that she was pregnant. That was the scariest to know as parents. Sam and I wondered, "How does she have the skills to take care of a child? How would she be able to finish school? How would she be able to get a job to financially support her baby?" Those thoughts about our daughter being pregnant was so stressful. She still didn't have a job, so she had no way to have the money to buy things for the baby. As a parent, I still worry about her and I always will.

Ashley wanted to keep the baby. However, we told her that she needed to find a job if she wanted to keep it.

"Remember," Sam lectured. "You will be raising this baby. This is your child and your child is first."

I spent as much time as I could teaching Ashley how to be a mother. I went over things with her such as how much it would cost to raise the child and what things she would need to buy for the baby. We made a list of things for the baby and how much they would cost. When Ashley got another job, she took that job seriously because she wanted to save money for the baby. She decided that it was time to smarten up and start making better decisions fo herself. when she was eight months pregnant, Sam and I took her shopping for baby clothes and other baby supplies.

When Ashley's baby was born, she weighed seven pounds and one ounce. Her length was twenty-two inches and she looked a lot like Ashley. She decided to name her baby Rebeca

Ashley decided to move back home so that she could save money to get her own place someday. She had to take time off of school to care for Rebeca. When Ashley worked, I would often babysit Rebeca. She worked part time because she wanted to be their for the baby as much as possible. Sam and I helped pay for the baby's diapers, baby wipes, and the crib while Ashley paid for the bottles and formula. For the most part, Ashley breast fed the baby.

After Rebeca was eighteen months old, Ashley decided to finish school so that she could find a good career. Sam and I congratulated her and told her how proud we were for her. She managed to get her GED and decided to go to a college to get a nursing diploma.

Carl's Funeral

(A sequel to Coming Out)
by Thomas Nguyen

Scene 1

(The setting is in Juliet's house. Francois and Juliet are sitting across from each other at the dining table. Francois speaks in a French accent.)
Francois: Bonjour Juliet, how are you today?
Juliet: Not well. I'm still grieving over the loss of my son and Gary doesn't give a shit about it.
Francois: I'm sorry to hear that Madam. I know it's hard.
Juliet: It is and I can't get over the fact that he is not here anymore. (Francois pats Juliet on the shoulder.)
Francois: He's in Heaven now Juliet. God will take care of him.
Juliet: I know, but he was too young. He had a future ahead of him and he was an honour's student through out grade school and university.
Francois: That's too bad. (Juliet looks at Carl's high school graduation photos hanging on the wall. She cries.) What's the matter?
Juliet: (Crying.) This was my son! He was so handsome and graduated with honours! He's not here anymore!
Francois: (Looking at the photos.) In deed he was. Just remember, if you remember him, he will always be alive in spirit and in your heart. God will take care of him. He's in a peaceful place hanging out with the angels and Jesus.
Juliet: (Tearing up.) Thank you Francois. (Gary enters the dining room.)
Gary: (Angry.) Juliet, get over your son! He was a big wuss and a fagot! He had no manhood because he chose to be gay.
Francois: (Firmly to Gary.) Don't talk to your wife like that! Don't forget that he's your son too and you should care about the fact that he committed suicide!
Gary: She's not my wife! We're divorced! I don't care about my son! I'm glad he disappeared! That fagot! (Juliet has a meltdown.) Juliet, don't be such a crybaby!
Francois: That's enough Gary! Don't ever come back or I will make you choke on your food!
Gary: Why do you care so much about Juliet?
Francois: I care about her because she is my friend! You're being very inconsiderate! Let me tell you something! You back off and choke on your food! (Francois forces Gary out of the house and locks the door.)

Scene 2

(There are three professors in the classroom. There are no students. Professor Ivy and Professor Richardson sit on either side of Professor Andrews. Professor Andrews is crying.)
Professor Andrews: (Crying.) I can't believe that Carl just took his life away like this! He was too young! He was a good student in my economics class!
Professor Ivy: I'm sorry that this happened Professor Andrews. You did the best you can. It's not your fault at all.
Professor Richardson: My chemistry 101 students and I tried our best to save him, but he couldn't be saved. I'm sorry too. (Professor Andrews takes some tissues and blows his nose. He wipes his tears.

Professor Ivy: (To Professor Richardson.) Poor Professor Andrews. I don't know what else to do.

Professor Richardson: Me too Professor Ivy.

Professor Ivy: Does the university know about Carl's death.

Professor Richardson: Yes they do. The news began to spread from student to student. Now, the whole university knows. An email was even sent about this. (Professor Andrews cries.)

Professor Andrews: I just don't know what to do! I just wish he didn't do this!

Professor Richardson: Nobody whats him to end his life. Even I was devastated when I found out that Carl could not be saved. Even the whole university was sad. (Professor Andrews sobs.)

Professor Ivy: (Checking her email.) Oh yes, I see the email you mentioned Professor Richardson. It also says that the university is going to have a memorial service for him. A scholarship will be named after him.

Professor Richardson: Correct.

Professor Ivy: It doesn't say when his memorial will be held,but the university will keep us up to date about this.

Professor Richardson: That is also correct. (Professor Ivy hands Professor Andrews tissues from her purse while he continues to cry.)

Professor Ivy: (To Professor Andrews.) Try to cheer up professor Andrews. Try to look at the positive side of things.

Professor Andrews: How am I supposed to do this Professor Ivy? It's so difficult to do when one of your students ended his life! He could have lived to be an economist! (Professor Ivy comforts Professor Andrews while Professor Richardson pats him on the back repeatedly.)

Professor Richardson: Try not to cry Professor Andrews. Remember that there are students in the school and we have to compose ourselves.

Professor Ivy: Professor Richardson, let him cry. He lost a good student of his. I would have felt the same way if this happened to me.

Professor Richardson: Okay, I understand.

Scene 3

(Cori, Zack, Megan and Rod are at Rod's house.)

Rod: Did you guys hear what happened?

Cori: We know about it Rod. We found him unconscious in the chemistry lab and tried to save him. There was nothing we could do because he was already dead.

Rod: Oh no, that's terrible.

Zack: After we told Professor Andrews, he began to become very emotional. He was crying non-stop. I hated to see a professor cry because it made me feel sad.

Cori: I had Professor Andrews for Economics 102 and he was a good Professor. I was one of Carl's classmates. He was a great contributor to the class because he always asked the professor questions. He got the fifth highest mark in the whole class. I nearly failed economics because I found the course to be difficult.

Rod: Oh, sounds like he did good. (Rod faces Megan.)) So Megan, how did you feel about this incident?

Megan: I was shocked and sad. I cried for days and I could not focus on my studies. So I dropped out of my spring classes before finals began.

Rod: I'm sorry to hear that. It must be hard dealing with a loss of someone you care about.

Megan: It is hard. I notified Juliet about the memorial service we are going to have at the university. She is going to be one of the speakers at the event.

Rod: Oh okay. I'll make sure to come to Carl's memorial. I had him as a room mate when we lived in the dorms. He was so much fun to hang out with. and he was unlike most nineteen year old guys. He was so mature.

Megan: I know he was. He was a good boyfriend. I dated him for a year. When he broke up with me, I was really sad. He told me that he was not attracted to women.

Rod: Oh, he did?

Megan: Yes.

Rod: (To Cori.) So Cori, how did you feel about Professor Andrews crying.

Cori: I was sad too. It was weird because I never seen a professor cry in front of students before. I did my best to comfort him, but it didn't seem to help.

Rod: Carl's death must have affected Professor Andrews a lot. He tried his best to help him get some professional help. I knew Carl's suicide plans because he told me about them.

Cori: I did not know until Professor Richardson showed me the suicide note that was in Carl's pocket.

Rod: Poor Professor Andrews.

Cori: I know. He was really upset. It made me and the other students sad. So, we cried along with him.

Scene 4

(Professor Ivy, Professor Andrews, and Professor Richardson are now in an office.)

Professor Richardson: Professor Ivy, I just got an email about when the memorial event. It's in three weeks.

Professor Ivy: Oh, that's good to know.

Professor Richardson: Are you going to go to the memorial?

Professor Ivy: Yes I am.

Professor Richardson: Oh, okay.

Professor Andrews: I'm going to go because Carl was a valuable student to have in the class room. He was so hard working and he got one of the top marks in the class.

Professor Richardson: Professor Andrews, I understand that it was sad losing one of your good students. He's in another place now.

Professor Andrews: I know, but he was too young. I was not ready to face his death at all. I felt hopeless after the students told me that he committed suicide.

Professor Ivy: I could tell how much it affected you because you were really emotional.

Professor Andrews: I don't know how to get over this. Finding out that your student killed himself is hard enough. Can you imagine that?

Professor Ivy: I sure can.

Professor Andrews: (Crying.) He was only nineteen years old! His life was too short! He will never be an economist like he dreamed he would be! If only he didn't kill himself! (Professor Andrews takes a tissue and wipes his tears.

Professor Ivy: (To Professor Richardson.) Poor Professor Andrews.

Professor Richardson: I know. He sure was really upset ever since he found out about Carl.

Professor Ivy: (Hugging Professor Andrews.) I know it's hard Professor Andrews, but we can't go back in time to stop this from happening. (Professor Andrews sobs.)

Professor Richardson: (To Professor Ivy.) I sure hate to see Professor Andrews cry. It's so sad. (Professor Andrews continues to cry while Professor Ivy continues to hug him. Professor Richardson hands him more tissues.)

Scene 5

(Francois, Juliet, and Gary are at Juliet's house. Francois is calm while Gary and Juliet are angry at each other.)

Gary: For goodness sake Juliet, get over Carl! I'm not going to his funeral and that's final!

Juliet: For goodness sake Gary, don't be so selfish! He is our son! You helped me create him!

Gary: He is not my fucking son anymore! He is a disgrace to the family by choosing to be gay!

Juliet: Oh please, you need to learn how to stop belittling our son! You're going to his funeral whether you like it or not!

Gary: You're not the boss of me! I don't have to go if I don't want to!

Francois: (Angry at Gary.) Gary, you are still Carl's father! You're acting very selfish right now! For goodness sake, this is 2016 not 1960! By the way, you should go to Carl's funeral and you need to accept that he was gay!

Gary: Whatever, I don't give a fuck! Cause Toi!

Francois: Well, you better care because he is your son and you should still love him for who he is! (Gary slaps Juliet and Juliet cries.) What is wrong with you? Never ever put your hands on Juliet! And never tell me to fuck off in French again!

Gary: I'm allow to hit a woman because I'm a man! Women are weaker than men are!

Francois: Get out! you are sexists and disgusting! (Gary leaves the house.)

Gary: Whatever, I will never come back ever again! (He slams the front door after he exits.)

Francois: (Comforting Juliet.) Juliet, I'm sorry about what Gary said.

Juliet: It's not your fault. By the way, thank's for standing up for me Francois.

Francois: It is my pleasure Juliet. I am your friend and that's what good friends do.

Juliet: So Francois, can I live with you in your condo? I have to sell my house because I can't afford it anymore.

Francois: Sure you can.

Scene 6

(A memorial is held at the university auditorium. The three professors, Iv, Richardson, and Andrews are in the audience. There are at least eighty students. Professor Andrews is crying. Cori is holding the mike. Rod and Megan are on the stage with Cori.)

Cori: Hello everyone, welcome to the memorial of Carl Mathews. As most of you know, he passed away last month. He was a good influence in Professor Andrew's Economics class. I was one of his class mates.

Professor Andrews: (Sobbing.) Professor Ivy, do you have any tissues? (Professor Ivy gives him some tissues.) Thanks. This memorial is so sad! It was like Carl died yesterday! I can't stop thinking about the time he said that he wanted to kill himself! This made me feel really sad!

Professor Ivy: I know how you feel. I understand that this was sad. (Professor Andrews continues to sob. Professor Richardson pats him on his shoulder.)

Professor Richardson: Please try not to cry Professor Andrews. You must be strong for Carl. The other students look up to you, so you must compose yourself.

Professor Andrews: It's easier said then done! It's not easy when you have a student who died, especially if he was a good student!

Professor Richardson: You will have other good students in the future. Right now, you must me strong for Carl. Please try to compose yourself. (Juliet enters the stage and Cori hands over the mike.)

Juliet: Hello, I'm Juliet. I would like to share some things about my son. He was an honours student for most of his school years. He was very hard working and had a full scholarship for his first year of university. I must say that his life was too short. He past away at the age of nineteen. (Professor Andrews continues to cry.) However, he will always be in my heart and I will always remember him. He will always be my son.

Professor Ivy: (To Professor Andrews.) Remember what Professor Richardson told you.

Professor Andrews: It's hard to get over this! The memory of Carl's death is so painful!

Scene 7

(Francois and Juliet are at Francois's condo.)

Francois: How do you like my condo Juliet?

Juliet: It's beautiful. Thank's for offering to have me live here.

Francois: How was carl's memorial?

Juliet: It was sad. There were a lot of tears in the audience.

Francois: I bet there was.

Juliet: There was this one man who kept crying constantly.

Francois: Oh, that must have been an emotional moment for him.

Juliet: His funeral will be next weekend. All of my relatives will be coming. You're welcome to come too.

Francois: Funerals are sad.

Juliet: I know they are. I just wish that my son was still alive. He's too young to die and have a funeral.

Scene 8

(Three months later.)

Francois: Juliet, will you marry me? (He puts an engagement ring on Juliet's left ring finger.)

Juliet: (Smiling.) Yes.

Francois: I really love you and I want you to be my future wife. (Francois kisses Juliet.

Juliet: I would love to be your future wife. I can't wait to tell my family and friends that you and I are engaged.

Francois: Me too. I'm sure Carl is very happy that you and I are going to get married. He's watching over you to make sure that you are healthy.

Juliet: How do you know that?

Francois: God told me. (A year later, Juliet is pregnant.)

Juliet: I have good news, I'm pregnant.

Francois: Really? That's exciting! Isn't thirty-eight years too old to be having a baby?

Juliet: No, I'm still young.

Francois: I'm just kidding Juliet. What is our baby's gender?

Juliet: I don't know. I've only been pregnant for three months. We will find out when I'm five months pregnant.

Francois: I can't wait to be a dad. I never had kids before. I would like to have two children.

Juliet: we'll try a year after our first child is born.

Rejection of a Transgender Son
by Thomas Nguyen

How is it like
To be a boy trapped in a girl's body?
It feels wrong.
My body is of one gender, while my mind is of the opposite gender.
I felt that way
Ever since I was twelve.

When I was a child, I was confused with my gender identity.
I didn't know why my mom put me in a dress
at five or six years of age.
When I was five, I lived in a foster home.
When I was in my foster brother's room,
I touched his private parts.
I didn't know why he had the genitals he had.
When I was in my own room, I explored my own genitals.
I noticed that they were different from his.
It was hard to understand.

When I was in Grade one,
my teacher had the boys say the months of the year.
Then, the girls did.
I would say the months of the year with the boys by mistake.
My aid, Janice, said to me,
"You're not a boy; you're a girl."
It took me until forth grade
To realize what boys and girls were.
I identified as a girl
Because I was told I was.

When I was twelve,
I began to menstruate.

It felt wrong and gross.
I started getting buds at nine and breasts at eleven.
At first, I thought I was a tomboy.
However, something was different; I wanted to be a boy.
I was not happy as a girl.

In high school, I was told to act more like a girl.
When I tried, it didn't make me any happier.
I tried things like wearing perfume and purses,
Thinking that it would make me feel more feminine.
After doing some research,
I began to realize
That I was transgender at nineteen.
I did not come out
Until I was twenty-two.

My professors were accepting of my transgender identity,
And so were my friends and sisters.
Mom had a harder time at first.
Then, she managed to understand.
She was very supportive.
If it weren't for them, I would not have continued to live
To complete my PhD in math to be a professor.
When I came out to my dad,
He was not accepting.
He did not take my transgender identity seriously.
I felt like committing suicide.
However, my math, physics, and economics professors did not want me
to do it.

To this day, I try to be strong.
I do not let anyone tell me that I am not a boy.
I am a boy.

Party Animal

Scene 1

Simon: Hi Hector, do you want to go and hang out at the bar on Saturday?

Hector: Sorry, I can't. I have to study for my midterms and finish my research paper.

Simon: Come on Hector, you have no life. You're always working and studying 24-7. Don't you want to relax once in a while?

Hector: But if I go to the bar, it'll throw me off my college schedule. Besides, my parents expect me to get straight A's. If I ever bring home a B, I'm dead.

Simon: Come on, it wouldn't hurt to just take a break once in a while. Besides, you deserve a break.

Hector: Okay Simon, I'll think about it. My parents are strict, so it is really hard to get them to let me go out.

Simon: Man, that sucks! I feel so terrible for you.

Hector: What am I going to do Simon?

Simon: Let's stay up until 2:00 in the morning doing homework until Saturday. We'll try to get it done before then. It'll give is time to go to the bar.

Hector: Okay, thanks Simon.

Simon: No problem bro. (Hector and Simon start on their homework. On the next day, Hector is in the living-room)

Hector: Hi mom and dad, I'm going to hang out with Simon on Saturday. We're going to the bar.

Dad: (In disapproval.) Absolutely not Hector! We don't want you to end up like the bad kids who waste their time drinking! You are going to study! End of story!

Mom: If you ever bring home another B, you are grounded for a month! You are going to spend time picking up horse poop and study 24-7. I don't care if you are tired!

Hector: (Protesting.) That is not fair! You guys never let me take breaks! every time I screw up, you guys always yell at me! Can't you just let me learn from my mistakes?

Dad: Look, life is about work! I came here from China to study university to complete my PhD so that I could be a professor! Your mom has put a lot of work into being a pharmacist! We want you to just finish school so that you can have a better life! Do you understand?

Hector: (Angry.) Life is more than just school! Don't you want me to have a social life and have friends? Don't you want me to at least work part time while in school? You guys think that life is all about school and you don't realize that it's about having a social life and gaining experience! You are the most unfair parents in the universe! I am going to move out and live with Simon in a dorm or apartment! I never want to speak to you guys again!

Dad: If you are going to talk to us like that again young man, then you can leave!

Hector: Fine! And by the way, I'm never speaking to you again you arrogant and absent-minded professor!

Scene 2

(The scene is in Simon's apartment.)

Hector: Hi Simon, my parents are incredibly mean! They don't even listen to anything I say; they just ignore me.

Simon: Dude, don't let it bother you. Be strong and proactive. Just try to ignore them back.

Hector: Man, I wish I knew how.

Simon: So Hector, what are your plans to get away from your strict parents?

Hector: I am going to move out and live with you. Is that okay?

Simon: Sure you can Hector. I have a spare bedroom that my old friend doesn't sleep in anymore. He is now living in a dorm.

Hector: (Excited.) Thank you Simon, you are the best!

Simon: No problem. That's what friends are for. We'll go to the bar after finals. Instead of going clubbing on Saturday, I can help you move your stuff.

Hector: Okay, we'll do it. (Hector exits Simon's apartment. The scene changes to his parents' house.)

Mom: Hector, can I talk to you for a second?

Hector: What do you want from me Mom? More studying?

Mom: It's not about that Hector, it's about you wanting to move out.

Hector: Look Mom, I'm nearly twenty years old. It's time for me to make my own decisions. You guys can't just control me for the rest of my life.

Mom: Your father and I don't want you to move out until you finish university. We pay for your tuition because we want you to go to school and be successful. Look, I don't want you to be a party animal like Simon. He's a bad guy. We yell at you because it's discipline. It's for your own good.

Hector: It's not fair discipline Mom; it's torture. You're just beating me up when I make a mistake. You never let me learn from failure. And by the way, Simon is not a bad guy. He also studies. He doesn't party all the time. You never even met him, so you can't judge him. I know him because I've been with him a lot, so don't you dare judge him if you don't know him.

Mom: Hector, focus on your studies first. Then, you can hang out with friends.

Hector: University is more than just studying. It's also important to make friends and socialize. I want to have friends while I'm in university; I don't want to wast my time being miserable. Look, I'm still going to move out. You may not like it, but it's time that I live on my own now. I'm an adult.

Mom: Do you understand that your father and I will miss you? I would be worried about you if you moved out? I wouldn't be able to take care of you.

Hector: Look Mom, I'm not ten; I'm nineteen. I'm old enough to take care of myself.

Mom: No matter how old you are Hector, you're still my baby. I hope you understand that.

Hector: I'm cutting off the umbilical cord now. It's time to let me go.

(Mom sobs while Hector exits.)

Scene 3

(Simon and Hector are in Hector's room. They are getting ready to pack.)

Hector: So Simon, do I need to bring my furniture?

Simon: Yes you do. Don't worry, I will call in a truck to move it. We'll start packing up your clothes and other possessions tonight. Then, we'll wake up and start moving stuff in tomorrow.

Hector: Okay, thanks man.

Simon: You're welcome Hector. So how do your parents feel about you moving out?

Hector: My mom was in tears. She did not want me to move out until I finish university.

Simon: she'll eventually get used to it. I moved out when I was your age Hector. I am now twenty-four years old. I am now in my fourth year of university and been living on my own for five years. It took a while for my parents to get used to me living on my own.

Hector: I hope that she won't be too worried. I want her to trust that I won't get into trouble.

Simon: She'll worry at first because she is not used to you living on your own. She needs time to get used to it Hector. Parents often find it hard to let their children grow up.

Hector; I wish that my mom would start realizing that I'm an adult and not a child.

Simon: She will Hector; it will just take time. Try not to rush her.

Hector: I don't know how to give her time to. I always rush her.

Simon: Look, a lot of moms worry about their kids. My mom still does, even though we don't see each other as often. She still wants her umbilical cord wrapped around you.

Hector: That bothers me a lot Simon.

Simon: I know how you feel Hector, but you must learn not to let it bother you.

Hector: I'll try my best Simon.

Simon: How do you feel about moving out?

Hector: I'm really excited. I can't believe that I will be starting my independent life. That's a big change for me.

Simon: Standing up to your parents and making the decision to move out was a very brief thing to do Hector.

Hector: Thanks.

Simon: I'm tired, lets go to bed.

Hector: Okay, I set my alarm early so we can have time to pack stuff and move out.

Simon: Good idea.

Hector: What time does the truck come tomorrow?

Simon: It comes at 1:00 in the after noon.

Hector: So are we going to pack my clothes and other stuff and move them in your car?

Simon: Yes.

Hector: Night Simon.

Simon: Night Hector. (Hector and Simon get ready for bed. The alarm goes off in the next morning. Simon and Hector wake up.)

Hector: Hey Simon, let's get packing so we can get out of here.

Simon: (Excited.) Okay, let's do it! Then, you can move into your new home! No more living with your overly strict parents! (Simon and Hector start to pack.)

Scene 4

(The scene is in Simon's apartment. All of Hector's stuff is still packed except his bed and dresser. They are in Hector's new room.)

Simon: Welcome to your knew home Hector.

Hector: Thanks Simon, I love my new room.

Simon: I'm glad you do.

Hector: I am so excited to start living here; I already feel like an adult.

Simon: That's good to here. Do you feel more happy now?

Hector: Yes I do Simon. I'm going to start unpacking my stuff now.

Simon: Would you like me to help Hector?

Hector: Sure you can. (Simon and Hector start unpacking.)

Living with a Visual Impairment

Thomas Nguyen

I have a visual impairment and I can only see shapes and basic colors like black, white, grey, and blue. The way I get around is not the way a sighted person get's around. I use a white cane to help me navigate. Growing up, this was what I had to learn to do.

There are pros to being visually impaired. I learned to not judge a book by its cover. I see people for their personalities and inner beauty. I find that sighted people focus too much on how a person looks. Also, I learned how to get around without the benefit of normal vision. I can do a lot of thins independently.

However, there are draw backs to being visually impaired. I'l never be able to get my driver's licence. However, that does not stop me. People look at me when I travel by myself and assume I need help. I encounter people who ask if I need help, but I also face people grabbing me out of nowhere. It scares me and annoys me because I don't like being grabbed. Imagine how you would feel as a visually impaired person. I bet you would not like that at all.

I often get asked by people about who cooks for me and how can I navigate by myself. I just tell them that I function just like everyone else, except I am visually impaired. People are also shocked when I tell them I live on my own. I think that most sighted people think that it would be hard for a visually impaired person to live on their own. However, they need to realize that it can be hard for anyone to live on their own, and not just people with disabilities.

Next, I will tell you the misconceptions that sighted people have about visually impaired people. They often assume that we have no vision and that we all have a white cane. Also, sighted people assume that we can only see black. However, not every person with visual impairments are totally blind. Most of us have some vision and not all of us use a cane. I also explain to sighted people that we have varying degrees of visual impairment.

Here are my pet peeves about sighted people. I hate it when they move things around without telling me. I find it frustrating because I rely on memory to know where things are. I also hate it when sighted people do not tell me when ever there is going to be something new in the house. Also, I find it annoying when sighted people leave their cupboards open because I can bump into them. They are a hazard to me. Also, I hate it when they make me play the guessing game. They expect me to know who they are when I only met them once. If I don't know who they are, they assume I forget them. But what sighted people need to know is that I only recognize people by their voice. I have to remind sighted people that they should identify themselves to me until I recognize their voice.

I have created a YouTube channel in 2012 to educate people about visual impairment. I explain the varying degrees of vision loss and how a visually impaired person lives their life. I also make videos on how I cope with my vision loss.

On Love
by Thomas Nguyen

Love feels great,
But it has its ups and downs just like a roller coaster.
Sometimes, love has its aches and pains
While at times, it is filled with warmth and joy.
We are blinded by love.
It is often easy to fall in love with the wrong people
Especially when we are young and naive.
We must choose our partners wisely.
They should be the person you have chemistry with,
But also compatibility.
A man often falls in love with a woman's appearance,
While a woman falls in love with his humour and personality.
Gentlemen, never try to attract a woman with money.
You must be congruent and authentic.
Women do not always like a man to buy her things.
If you do this, you will end up in her friend zone.

Millennials Suck! by Thomas Nguyen

If you don't know what a millennial is, I'll tell you. A millennial is someone who is born

during the 1980's or 1990's. This generation is known to be self-entitled and self centred. This

generation is also called 'generation Y", as in, "why is this generation so spoiled?". Why are we

dependent on X? I mean Generation X.

I must confess. I'm a millennial myself. I was born in the 1990's. In fact, early 1990's.

This is my perspective on the millennial generation.

Growing up, I was unaware of how people were grouped into categories based on there

generation. I didn't think too much about what a difference it made. A few years after I became a

legal adult, I started noticing that more and more people in my generation were refusing to grow

up. I wondered why. I did research on the internet and red peer reviewed articles. They suggested

that because more and more millennials were finding it hard to get a job, We choose to live at

home. It makes sense financially. Also, I'm okay with people choosing to live at home. Just as

long as they do things around the house and not act like a couch potato. However, if we stay at

home during our early adult years, we won't be able to learn how to cope in the real world.

Also, my generation is the biggest generation of boomerangs and wusses in my opinion.

A lot of us did not learn to develop the coping skills needed to deal with college and life after

school. I think we're the Petter Pans in the 20t century. This is why I can''t stand my generation.

I avoid acting like most millennials. I don't want to be one of the chumps like a lot of

people my age. First of all, I hate being coddled and babied. It's not going to do be anything in

the long run. I would be raised for failure, not success. In university, I would not succeed because I wouldn't have developed the maturity to deal with university life. I would be afraid to step out of my comfort zone. I always want to challenge myself and step out of my comfort zone so I can grow and mature as an individual. I think that life is a meritocracy. You get what you deserve. If you want to achieve in life, you have to put in effort and stick to your goals. If you don't put in any work, you don't get good results. It's like studying for a test. You get the grade that you deserve.

In a YouTube video, "Helicopter Parents Hovering Over the College Campus", a college consultant explains about parents calling their child's professors to complain that their child is not getting an A or B.. That makes no sense to complain about this. It's so stupid and pathetic. It's like saying, "Professor so and so, my child deserves a B or A regardless of their effort." Also, parents intervene in the child's life to much. They jump in a problem solve for their child when he or she has roommate problems. The cell phone then becomes the umbilical cord between the parent and the adult child. The child expects his or her parents to problem solve for him/her. When the child calls them several times a day, he or she would ask, "Mom, dad, I have a problem with my class. It's so stupid. How do I get out of this class? How do I avoid this professor?" Then, the parents white knight for the adult child. They become like manjinas.

Now that Generation Z and Alpha are around, we need to set an example for them. We need to stop being entitled and spoiled brats. I don't want Generation Z to look at my generation and say, "Wow, people older than us are losers." We must learn how to develop good coping strategies so we can be more effective as individuals. We should crave success instead of striving for equal outcome or equity.

Teen Pregnancy

by Thomas Nguyen

I had a classmate in my high school class who was pregnant. She was seventeen years old. To be honest, at that time, I thought of her as irresponsible for getting pregnant young. I thought to myself: "She's not even married and she is having a kid." I often judged other teenagers for getting pregnant young. After all, they're children having children. They're still in school and under the care of their parents.

Shows such as "Teen Mom", and "16 and Pregnant" normalize teen pregnancy like it's not a big deal. It's a concern to me because i worry that other teens would want to get pregnant to be on TV. First of all, they don't have the maturity to care for a kid, let alone they're still kids themselves. They're not women yet; they are still girls. They have a lot of growing up to do. When I watched "Teen Mom", and "16 and pregnant", I observed that teen dads often run away from their responsibilities. They're not men; they're boys. They leave the girls to be single parents. They can't even financially support themselves, let alone a child.

I have concerns about babies being born to teen moms. They are more likely to be born premature. Adolescent mothers' bodies are still developing and they can end up with fistula. Babies born to teen moms are more likely to grow up in poverty. Daughters of teen moms are more likely to become pregnant as teenagers themselves. Children born to teen moms are more likely to drop out of school.

Teen moms are more likely to drop out of school. Also, they are more likely to live on welfare. Also, teen dads are less likely to stick around to help raise the baby. So, teen moms end up being single parents. Most of them do not have the maturity to be moms. Their brains are still developing. They also need to finish school so they can better themselves.

Although I have another friend who is still in school and raising her kids, I recommend to wait until you finish your education first. Also, it's important to be financially stable so you can have the money to bring up a child. That way, the child does not grow up in poverty. Personally, I think that people should be married first before having children. I also don't think that sex should be out of wedlock. However, if teens choose to have sex, they should wait until they are mature enough to understand the consequences. Also, they need to be educated about how to use birth control and other contraceptives correctly. Even though you are using birth control, there is still a small chance that pregnancy can occur. Condoms brake. A girl could miss her birth control pill. She can also lie about being on the pill. Once she is pregnant, it's going to change her life. This means no more hanging out with her friends, going out, and doing other things that other teens do.

My advice to boys and young men is to not way your life down by getting your girlfriend pregnant. They need to figure out who they are and find a stable job. Young men need time to mature, especially in their teens and early twenty's. Their brains take longer to mature then women's brains. Although men do not have to worry about pregnancy, the mothers can make they pay child support for the next eighteen years.

Does Babying Help?

by Thomas Nguyen

During my teenage years, my mother was overprotective because of my visual

impairment. She expected very little from me. I was not allow to go anywhere by myself and use

the stove. Because of my visual impairment, she saw me as a person who was not normal and as

some one that needed to be felt sorry for.

In high school, I was so tired of of mo mother sheltering me. I wanted to be more

independent. I felt like I needed to rebel a bit. I'm very fortunate that my aid in high school have

encouraged me to take risks. Her name was Angela Roppo. Donna Konschuh, my aid from

Junior high, kind of babied me, but it wasn't to the point that my mom babied. I started taking

the ETS by myself. It took practice until I got the hang of it. My father was okay with me

learning how to take the bus. On the other hand, my mother had a hard time letting me ride the

bus by myself. She was scared that I would get lost.

Overtime, I learned how to travel independently to work and school. It really raised my

confidence. This was empowering to me as a person with a visual impairment because I had a

way that I didn't have to always rely on some one for transportation. This gave me the freedom

to go wherever I needed to go.

Gradually, my mom began to trust me with taking the bus by myself. To this day, she is

proud of me for my independence. She does not baby me anymore. I'm really proud of her for

supporting me to be independent. On the other hand, if I was still babied to this day, I would not

have the maturity and confidence to make it through adulthood. I would not have developed the skills for university and independent living. So, in the long run, babying would not help me; it would cripple me even more.

What I would advise to parents is not to baby their children. It doesn't do any good. If parents baby, they would raise incapable adults. They would be setting their children up for failure, not for success. Trust me, professors do not want college and university students who are coddled. Also, professors don't want to hear from parents who complain that their child is not getting an A or B. In university, we're treated like adults. There are higher expectations and students need to have the maturity to deal with university life.

If parents, especially the mothers, cook and do everything for their children, it will also cripple them. When the children become adults, They would have no idea how to cook, clean, grocery shop, and other essential things for survival in the adult world.

I'm Dating my University Professor

by Thomas Nguyen

I'm currently in my second year of university. I'm doing a bachelor of arts with a major in Psychology and a Sociology minor. I have a crush on one of my sociology professors. I've been staring at him ever since the beginning of my second year. He seemed very demanding in the lecture hall and had a strong sense of authority. He also seemed very knowledgeable. That was what I found attractive about him. His name was Professor Stevenson. He is in his early thirties.

When I told my mom that I had a crush on a professor and was dating him, she disapproved. She was not happy to hear that. She looked at me and said, "Jordan, that is not cool. I'm not okay with you dating one of your professors."

"Why? Age is just a number. Him and I are both adults. What's the big deal?"

"That's not the point," my mom continued. "It's never going to be an equal relationship. He was your professor. He was in charge of grading you in his class."

My mom continued to lecture me about it for another thirty minutes. I'm tired of her telling me who to date and who not to date. I'm nineteen years old. She talks to me like I'm still a little kid. After my eighteenth birthday, I was hoping that she would not treat me like an adult, but no.

I've started dating my professor by the end of my first semester. We've been staying at hotels and went for drinks. We also went out for dinners. My professor also paid for everything, including new purses and shoes. I throw out the dinner and hotel receipts at the hotel rooms because I don't want my mom to find out that my professor and I were going to dinners and hotels. She would do anything to stop me from dating him. She's crazy and overprotective. If she finds out, she might try to ground me.

My mom does not know that I have lost my virginity to my professor. I had sex with him quite often in the hotel rooms. Him and I make sure to use birth control. I always make sure he wears a condom. I take birth control daily because I don't want to get pregnant. I'm not ready to be a mom yet.

Another reason why I take birth control is because I get very irregular periods. In high school, my mom took me to see a doctor to have birth control pills prescribed to me. I've been taking them for three years. They help me regulate my period.

I have a plan in case I find out I'm pregnant. My plan is to get an abortion. I have emergency contraceptive pills. I take them right after I have sex. I know that birth control is not perfect and it is important to have back up birth control.

Next year, I'm going to another university. I currently go to the University of Alberta. I want to go to the University of Calgary to finish my degree. I'm planning to live in a dorm because I'm tired of living under my mom's rules. I'm going to work full time in the summer so I can save up for my living expenses. Also, it would be weird staying at the University of Alberta because I'm afraid that other professors and students would find out that Professor Stevenson and I are dating. I told him about my plan to move to Calgary and he was very supportive about it. My mom, in contrast, tried to convince me to live at home for university. I told her that I wanted to study in Calgary instead.

Professor Stevenson prefers students to call him by his first name. He says that "Professor" sounds too formal. He goes by Bill. On our dates, he wants me to call him "Bill" and not "Professor." So that's what I do. Also, he does not like to be called "Doctor." I called him "Doctor" the first time I had him as a professor. He said, "Just call me by my first name. It feels awkward when I'm called 'Doctor'. I just want to keep it less formal." So, for the rest of the term, that was what I did.

I'm almost done my second year of university. After exams are over, I'm going to live with Bill until I have to Calgary to study. I've already got accepted into the University of Calgary. I did not tell my mom that I was going to live with Bill in an apartment. He was selling his house because he didn't want to pay mortgage anymore.

Bill is single. He has no children of his own. He is hoping to start a family some day. He is currently in his early thirties. He is not the creepy old professor that I thought he was.

When Bill and I started dating, news of this began to spread to the other faculty in his department. They criticized him for being unprofessional. Other students heard about it too. They accused me for being a gold digger and Bill for being a pervert. They said things to me such as: "Why are you dating a professor? He's probably a petifile. You're just a teenager."

I told them to mind their own business and they should not tell me who to date. Besides, I'm legally an adult. So I can date Bill. Also, if my mom finds out that I'm moving to Calgary with Bill, she would try to stop this from happening. Apparently, I found out that she has been looking through my phone while I was sleeping. I was mad at her and said that it was an invasion of my privacy.

"I am your mother Jordan. It's still my job to protect you. You're still a kid," she said. "I don't want anything bad to happen to you."

"Mom, I'm a legal adult!" I yelled. "I'm tired of you trying to control me! I'm not a kid anymore and I pay my own cell phone Bill! So you can't just look at my phone!"

"Listen, you still live in my house, so I set the rules. You're going to do what I say. I said no dating your professor. Find a boy your age to date. You'll have a lot more in common with a boy closer to your age."

I don't like dating guys my age. They're so immature. They don't even have their shit together at all. They lack manliness and still expect me to lead the relationship. I like to date older guys. They're more likely to be financially stable and have more wisdom than some twenty-two year old boy. My professor is mature and he has his own house. However, he's going to live in an apartment so he does not have to pay mortgage anymore. Once he sells his house, he would use it to pay the rest of the mortgage.

I asked Bill if he was going to find a job in Calgary as a professor at another university. He said yes. He will resign his job at anthem University of Alberta and apply for a position at the University of Calgary. I will not go to that university because it would create some ethical issues. I will study at Athabasca University because I want to be able to balance work with school.

However, Bill seems to have a plan to start a family in a few years. I told bill that I didn't want to get married until I finish school. I mentioned to him that I wanted to do my Master's degree in psychology so I could become a psychologist. Bill was supportive of what I wanted to do with my career. He was also fine with me working to pay for school. He understands how expensive university is. So he suggested that I apply for as many scholarships as possible. He

offered to help me apply for any grant or scholarship that I would be qualified for.

Made in the USA
San Bernardino, CA
12 June 2020